The Power in Your Posture

Activating the power within you to discover the CEO in you!

Theo A. Chunn Jr.

Editors:

Evelyn M. Chunn & Camry Wilborn

ISBN: 1984226770
ISBN-13:978-1984226778

Dedication

I would like to dedicate this book to my beautiful wife Evelyn Michelle (my best friend, queen and partner in ministry) who has supported this vision since the day we met. Thanks for the extra push and enhansing my vaule by allowing me to be the man I am and the ablity to be surrounded by your natural beauty daily. To my awesome rockstar childern Gracelynn and Theodis III their support is outstanding. Being honored to be chosen by God, to be their father has truly made my life complete. It is because of them that I have a purpose to grow personally, professionally and academically. To my wonderful mother Annice, thank you for showing me better than telling me, the ways in which I can grasp all of my goals. Dad Theodis, thanks for imparting in me wisdom and courage to surpass every obstacle that I face. My Sisters (Laketia, Inez, Laura, Takisha, Kiana and Kiara) Brothers, (Gyrod, Elroy, Joseph, Travis and Sean) Thank you for being the family I needed- your support is outstanding and priceless. I thank every student, colleagues and friends (especially Dr. Kathy Stitts, Dr. Michael Magruder, Mrs. Kimberly Reese, Ms. Dale Williams, Mrs. Letitia Wall and so many others) of Winston-Salem State University. Thanks to Apostle Nicole Bonds and the Life Nation Family for encouraging me to take a leap of faith. Last but not least I want to thank my spritual father Bishop Hezekiah Pressley and the New Beginnings Ministry family for pushing me to this level!

CONTENTS

INTRODUCTION

ACTIVATE THE POWER WITHIN YOU!

"You're only measured in terms of success, by his investment in terms of contribution" – Bishop T.D. Jakes

So many times we start something but hardly ever finish what we started. For example, I began writing this very book about five years ago, and every time I started it, I quit after every paragraph. It came to the point that over time I just completely gave up. At the same time, I kept pushing everyone around me to complete their dreams. Sometimes as a motivational speaker, you will push others to live a more victorious life and learn to settle with your own lifestyle. Today, I make a stand as I write the dream down and give it its own heartbeat. Today I stand against procrastination and move beyond the thoughts, the dreams, the desires, and the goals.

Have you ever thought to yourself, I could be and I should be in a better place (financially, personally and professionally) in this thing called life? Well, what if I told you that the same amount of time that we have, is the same time a successful person has. What makes the successful person successful is what they do with the time that they are provided with on a daily basis. Every day we must take our goals by the hand and breathe life into them. In Genesis when God made man, he created humans in his own image (Genesis 1:27). However, they were just created beings until God breathed into them (Genesis 2:7). Sometimes we have to understand that a dream is just that- a dream if it has no breath. A desire is just a desire without it. And a goal is just a goal if you have not breathed on it.

Life is waiting for you to realize that potential is within you. There is no reason to ask permission to utilize what's already in your possession. Each day that we're allowed to "try it again" we should do it with everything within us. When God gives you the ability to wake up again, He gives you the gifts and access that you need to get it done. With every dream, you must demand it to have life. We do that by simply calling it and breathing on the very thing we want to come to pass. If I told you that God is actually waiting to see if you're able to utilize what you have before opening up the windows of heaven, in order for you to live in your blessings, would you take care of what's in front of you?

The access that we have been desiring is already within us. The same YES that you gave God years ago activates the very thing that is concerning you now. I was listening to a YouTube video of Bishop T.D. Jakes and Pastor Steven Furtick, and Bishop Jakes analyzed something that activated a fresh start within me. He said, "God doesn't make chairs, for God gave us the brain, and the brain will develop an idea that will look at a tree and create the chair." He later said that the church has created people to think and ask God for furniture while God is saying, "I don't do that, I make trees." This absolutely blew my mind. For years I have been asking the earth to provide something to me that I already had. You have to admit to yourself, your dreams are priceless, and if you had actually worked that one dream and breathed on it and gave it life, you would be in a different world right now. I encourage you to tell yourself right now, at this very moment "THE WAIT IS OVER." You have to encourage yourself out of your lazy mentality and into the CEO you really are.

When you pass by cemeteries, they are filled with many dreams, desires and even goals that individuals wanted to

9

complete, but life got the best of them. I was talking with a dear friend of mine, and I said to them "you know worrying will kill you." The mere fact that we are always trying to find the solution. We have the dreams and goals, but it's the next step that pushes us into the worrying mode. I have read many books about stepping out on faith, and how to grasp your goals, but they never mentioned that worrying about how the dream unfolds will literally kill you. As I allowed that statement to sink in, we agreed to make a pledge that our dreams will live for themselves and that we would ensure that our dreams would not meet the grounds of a cemetery.

Defined Posture

When I was growing up, people would've thought my sister and I were raised by a military family. Not because we traveled a lot (which we did), but based on our very strict and stern posture. My mother would often inform us if our posture was incorrect. We were afraid humps would form in our backs. Thirty years later, I didn't think I would be sitting down, writing a book on effective posture. It's amazing how the word itself has transformed in so many ways. Throughout the growing stages of life, our posture becomes strengthened and should grow stronger and stronger as life progresses. Now older and actually having a family of my own, I am quickly understanding that all this time I have had the motivators, the encouragers, and the drive to be successful. The one thing I kept overlooking was the desire to **push myself**, **encourage myself**, **motivate myself** and set the right and precise posture to be all and achieve all.

As a student in grade school, I was not the best student academically, but teachers would always tell my mother during parent-teacher conferences that I was a bright student with great potential to succeed- but I needed to put more drive and dedication towards my academics. I can remember one of my elementary school teachers Mrs Pat Lewis. I would cry if I saw her name as my teacher for the following year. I felt as though she would request to have me as a student. Looking back on those days, she was the only one in that school who could push me towards greater. What's sad is that my children may not ever come in contact with a teacher like Mrs. Pat Lewis.

Mrs. Pat Lewis' sternness in class remained with me throughout life and prepared me to be great. The one time I was paddled (yes, I am old enough to remember paddling) changed my entire life. It wasn't the fact that I was being paddled that caused my embarrassment. It was in that moment that I realized I had to maintain a certain posture. I also realized that I had let my family down and as a man. The purpose I had as a king had to be awakened, and I had to breathe life again. I did not understand that I was simply existing and not living out my fullest potential.

Years later my mom, sister, and I moved to North Carolina, and this was my time to step up. I was connected to other family members who were motivators and those who could support my family in ways we couldn't imagine. It was like an angel lifted us up and moved us over fifteen hours away from our original home. I remember going to school on the first day looking at all of the teachers' names. I wanted to make sure Mrs. Pat Lewis didn't follow me to North Carolina. However, I was searching for someone who had the heart to go beyond teaching and push me even further. I finally saw myself strengthening my posture-actually my entire family was doing the same thing. The posture of my family was effectively strengthening and healing. My mom was able to live out her dream and become a police officer while my sister and I began college. By the time I was ready to enter college, I was fully ready to become the best man I could honestly be.

Throughout my life, I have had some remarkable opportunities that not only pushed me – but the majority of them challenged me to be a better person. Some of my worst days turned out to be encouragement which led to my best days. Those individuals who were key players in discouraging me didn't know that they were actually pushing me towards greater. Today I stand as an academically committed young man- a King who understands where he needs to go and equally knows how to seek guidance to successfully obtain professional advisement.

Transforming Challenge into Purpose

For years I thought Mrs. Pat Lewis was my worst enemy. I thought she had it out for me- but instead, I was the lucky one. She really liked me and wanted more for me. I don't really know if Mrs. Pat Lewis is still alive, but if she is I need to really find her and say "Thank you." Ms. Dale Williams was my advisor while I served as Mister Winston-Salem State University at Winston-Salem State University. Ms. Williams was stern, professionally strict, and serious about pushing students to the next level. You would think that someone who had a teacher like Mrs. Pat Lewis would be able to identify that Ms. Williams was only there to protect, guide, direct and most importantly advise me to my destiny. Let me ask you a question, have you ever assumed that you knew more than you really did? Well, you don't know it all! Many times in life we run from direction, even if it will push us farther and closer to our fullest potential. Here is a bit of advice - successful people listen to advice, take criticism, and apply their notes to develop into an even more successful person. While others run slightly not looking back, yet thinking they know it all.

I remember listening to Sheryl Underwood on the View. She was explaining a conference call she was on and how the others on the call were talking about her and the comments were not good. She said she could have done a lot of things, but in the midst of her getting mad, she encouraged herself to write down some notes. Sometimes we have to put our feelings to the side and really listen to the constructive coaching so that we can reach our fullest potential. There has to be a desire within you that pushes every excuse, every doubt and every fear to the side to become that person you always dreamed of being. Dreams are magical moments that gives you a glance at the potential within you. Let's birth out those desires, purposes and outstanding lifestyles that we've been longing for.

I remember when I was in high school, I auditioned for American Idol. I envisioned my life to change for my whole family. I mean it came right to my backyard, Charlotte, NC. I walked in, tried to remember the song and forgot the words. Later, I would tell my mom that I just had to go to New York and audition. I was about 16 or 17 years old, and even to this day, I am surprised my mom allowed me to travel alone to seek a dream. Needless to say, I didn't make the cut. The judges said I had a gospel voice. I traveled back to North Carolina by train with the same dream and a non-quitting spirit. I auditioned one last time in Georgia. I traveled to Georgia with my mom. This was the same season that North Carolina's own Fantasia would win American Idol. The judges would say the same thing as they did in New York, "great voice but not what we're looking for." I was so devastated- but deep down inside I still had a desire to be great. Even though allowing others to judge your talent can sometimes shatter your confidence, you have to look to those who push and motivate you. I don't think my mother would have encouraged me to travel, stay in line and put myself out there for others to judge if she didn't believe in me. Even at this very moment, I collect the energy I had then to push and challenge me to the next level now.

The Power in your Posture provides personal advice on how to use your past and current situations to position you for an effective posture academically, professionally and spiritually. This book is purposed to push you into your next level, which will prepare you for the ultimate form of promotion and propel you into destiny. Throughout the pages of this text, you will do a lot of self-evaluation which will help tear down the walls of insecurity, self-doubt, and confidence. Who can we depend on to motivate us, inspire us, encourage us or push us? We must do the pushing- We must do the encouraging... WE MUST DO THE MOTIVATING" Let this literature be the push that motivates you to greatness and 100% Success!

"May he grant your heart's desires and

make all your plans succeed."

-Psalms 20:4

CHAPTER ONE

The Self-Assessment

Life is too short for you to give up on yourself! Stop quitting and keep pushing! Make today count.

Have you ever noticed how fast the months, weeks, and days go by? It's simply amazing (and somewhat scary) that time flies by extremely fast. With that being said, we don't have time to just dream about where we want to be in life. Most failures happen because we allow "failure" to take place. There is another part of failure that we will get to in a later chapter which pushes us into position for our next season. Today, I want to encourage you to work on "self," take time to examine your failures (and all that you believe to be a weak area in your life) and use it to push yourself by identifying those specific things that make you happy. We work on things for others daily but rarely do things that make us happy or grow. I'll ask the question again, when was the last time you had a meeting about yourself, for yourself?

Today is the day to get it right, today is the day to MAKE IT COUNT!

As we grow older holidays, birthdays and the reoccurrence of the seasons seem to get closer and closer. When we were children it was something we looked forward to- It's amazing how throughout life we stopped growing, stopped having the desire to grow and our energy level dropped, and we ultimately quit. Quit dreaming, quit visioning and quit thinking about the greater that is within us. This is somewhat a part of the evolution of life right? We are created, born, and we grow, and eventually, it becomes our time, and we leave. If you have ever worked around or even lived around an elderly person who is up in age, you will witness a slow paced in mobility and speech. They somewhat transform back into their infancy stage- some needing more assistance than others. Well, I personally believe if we exercise our minds and our dreams to never stop growing and going and always pushing ourselves to greater then we will see the fruits of our labor ensuring that we write a different outcome for our latter years. I have always thought that when I'm 90 years old that I will just begin to look like I'm 40. Jokingly, I desire to be young in my ideas, thoughts, and innovation of what I create and deliver. Again, WE must MAKE it COUNT!

That leads me to ask this question. What is your "IT"? In life, we have so many dreams, aspirations and so-called purposes and missions for our lives that we end up quitting our IT. I truly believe that once we identify our "IT" we will be able to live life more abundantly. If you're ready for a new place and to reach your truest potential you will have to understand that "Your" dreams and "Your" goals are not your God-given abilities. What you've been dreaming about may just be a puzzle piece to the grand master plan. Sometimes we focus on what we think is the master plan, and it's only a stepping stool to that place where God wants us to be. As we are getting equipped for our new season, I want to encourage you to get connected and align your missions, dreams aspirations to what God has effectively mapped for you and take that and run with it. It will take you to higher places than you ever imagined.

To ensure that I never lose focus on being the best me I can be, I love doing what I call the "self-assessment" on who I am compared to who I used to be, compared to who I want to become. Remember this is still aligned with the person God has called me to be. You can't get to the self-assessment and still not know what you're assessing because you are clueless about what God called you to specifically be. I encourage you to find that purpose first and then assess afterward. Just take a moment and think about the many dreams you had as a child- how has that changed now? Many times we have come across something or someone who has denied us. This has caused us to deny ourselves. Spiritually we must build upon our childhood dreams- we think we have transitioned beyond our dreams, but they are still somewhat there. If you ask your boss or those who influence you what their childhood dreams were, I guarantee you there are in a field very close to their dream. The focus we had and the desire we encountered to just simply dream as children are amazing. Take for instance that you lived the dreams you had as a child? Oh how living the edge you would be doing? Some of the dreams take courage to think it, live it, do it and actually achieve it. One thing that gets me even today is the fear of doing/ living that particular dream. I have had the thought for years to quit my job. But I keep thinking I have a wife and two children- what will happen if I don't get the income that I need to provide for my household. Our dreams are connected to the God-Given desires, therefore if He gave them to you, why not trust HIM enough to understand that He will get you through and He will provide.

Once you examine who you are and build upon what is possible of whom you are- the push begins. Prepare while understanding the need to succeed and be happy in the process. The preparation stage of the "Push Process" allows one to plan out every method and strategy to assess your personal mission and purpose. After you plan effectively and have shared knowledge with ideal resources on how you can accomplish your dreams, then you create reachable outcomes and measurable goals. The understanding becomes evident when the plan is realistic as well as Godly possible (and we know that ALL things are possible with GOD). The desire to be successful lies within each individual who walks on this earth. I don't believe anyone says I just want to be a failure. If so, you possibly need to stop reading and motivate your "self" quickly. Ultimately, when you are able to effectively plan, understand who you are, and be successful in your doing you will be happy with what you do and who you are. While pursuing my doctoral degree, I had to take a course entitled "Strategic Planning." While in the class I thought about how I could personalize this and make my life work better. In order to plan, you must first have a vision and a mission of what you want to accomplish. After you have something that is concrete and stable to withstand the economy, your future, and who you want to become; you can begin the process. Many times we just begin with the end in mind which is great- but we don't realize or put into perspective everything and lose focus on the vital aspects of the planning process. The planning process is vital to the success of our being. If you have children or desire to have a family, it can also position them and even their children for a better life.

Within the personal strategic plan you will need to do a SWOT (Strengths, Weakness, Opportunities, and Threats) analysis, and in order to be effective in doing that, you will need some outside realistic strengths, weaknesses, opportunities, and threats in which you are currently performing. This will bridge the gap and increase your personal, professional and scholastic growth. In most cases, this is where our development of the self-assessment ends, due to the simple fact that we think what we're doing is right in all aspects. There are several things that I do as a man, husband, father and employee that I know I need to change- however, having others within those areas assess my performance provides a better gauge at what I need to personally work on. For example, I constantly ask my wife if there anything I need to work on as a husband. This is not to say that I'm not confident in my relationship- I just need to know from her point of view if I am doing everything she wants her husband to do. This brings up a very good point because marriage is a job and if you are inconsistent now being single you may not be ready to go further as it relates to marriage. Just like there are yearly assessments on the job- we have to assess our personal lives the same.

Also creating a proposed budget will ensure that your financial "self" is meeting the standards that you desire. TD Jakes once said in a sermon about making your wallet meet up with your dreams, not your dreams meet up with what's in your wallet. In order to make your dreams to reality in a big way, you must plan it to work out. Take Tyler Perry, for instance, we all know his story of how he was homeless living out of a car and just continued to produce plays- I don't personally think he would be where he is if he hadn't planned to be where he is now. Thinking outside of the box and ensuring that you are doing everything possible to be great is the most important aspect of this process.

Let's make it clear that the process is never meant to be a pretty process. Take a house, when a contractor builds a house they have to move around the dirt and most of the times the work building the house is not the prettiest scene. Sometimes we fail at sticking with the process. The world has made everything so convenient that we believe the process is supposed to be microwavable. Listen, you're not going to get anywhere in life without going through something. You have to go through to get to your destiny. I want to encourage you at this moment that you are going through so much just to see if you are ready and equipped for greater! Just continue to go through so you can see beyond your right now.

During my experience as an academic coach, I often tell my students "don't just go to class as the student- go to class as the expert, the one who engages and takes control of their status in the classroom." We live in a classroom daily, but it depends on how your posture is set up and how you take control of where you're going in life. We can all be great at something, most importantly our creator has developed us and planned the world for us to be spectacular in our own unique way. Some take advantage of it while others are just sitting on their gifts allowing life to be very normal and possibly dull. I know, life for me has had its dull moments- but when I think about where I'm going now, I can truly say it will never be dull again. I can tell you now that I speak that simple phrase over my life. I will NEVER LIVE DULL Moments, nor will I share my thoughts, dreams, and plans with DULL PEOPLE!

If you have ever quit something, don't call it a failure, simply call it THE PROCESS. Sometimes within the process, there are things that cause us to pause for so many reasons. Also for those Christians, you can't blame everything on the devil. I will remind you of the book of Job where the Lord asked Satan have you considered my son and servant Job? Basically, the Lord gave Satan "permission" to touch him. Everything in life is not the devil trying to steer us away from doing right- it's simply a process and a test to see if we can stand the storm for the blessings to shower down on us. The moral to that small but vital story- Stop blaming those who have NO control over you- simply go through the process with your head held high and knowing that there is something GOOD which will come after this storm.

Several things cause us to quit something or shall I say pause our personal movie, however, we don't have time to just stay there- we must understand that it is a process so we must get back up and go! Take the process of a caterpillar into a beautiful butterfly it takes a process. Just the other day my wife, daughter and I ran a 5k, and we saw a lot of caterpillars and my wife was grossed out. I started to think about their process (similar to our individual process). The journey begins with a caterpillar hatching from an egg scientifically termed as Larva. Then the caterpillar fills itself up with leaves growing bigger and longer through a series of molts in which it sheds its skin. The caterpillar stops eating and hangs itself upside down from a tree limb or leaf and spins itself in a cocoon. Within the protective temporary habitat, the caterpillar transforms its body becoming a butterfly. We, like the butterfly, have our own process of being transformed. Understanding your process is much different than my process, or your colleague's process. This is why assessing your failure, weakness or pause will help you discover your process and allow you to build and redevelop your centered-driven mission. The quitting process is not meant to stop you- it's meant to press pause, redevelop and fast forward to your success!

With self-evaluation, there has to be a time where you restore confidence back to the original birthing place. Just think about when you were born, and as infants, we would believe we could do anything we saw. Sometimes, I just stop what I'm doing to look at my two children (Gracelynn 2 years old and Theodis III is 1 years old). They have so much confidence in the world. They supply a new level of energy and confidence into me daily. I mean it amazes me that every day they try something new and even if they failed the day before or even an hour before they would still try to do it again. Today, I ask that you go back and reconnect your fearless ways to your now. I mean it's like playing the lottery, some don't hit the jackpot with the first ticket, but there is hope and faith within you that keeps you going back in hopes that someday you will have the winning ticket. What if I told you, today was your chance? The chance to earn all that you have purposely sowed into the ground; the chance to outlive your dreams and desires. Well, guess what, today is the day, and it starts with the mindset.

When was the last time you dreamed?

Secondly, when was the last time you really worked on that particular dream? Well, it's time to WAKE UP!!! You're closer than you think!

CHAPTER TWO

The Making of the Millionaire Dollar Mindset

Today is a brand new day! It's time for you to wake up from your dreams and actually start putting your dreams on paper and working those dreams out so that they could actually be a reality. Have you ever thought that you have been dreaming for a long time and your dreams are still waiting for you to accomplish them? The time is now, wake up and smell the success. I remember a time when I was able to accomplish almost every dream that I had. For instance, before I started college I knew I wanted to be a drum major for a historically black college and university, more specifically Winston-Salem State University. After two years in the band, I was able to accomplish that goal. Going forward I had a goal to become Mister Winston Salem State University, and I was able to make that goal come true. As time passed, I begin to get too comfortable with my dreams that I stopped pursuing them, and really this is an energy that if you don't get better with using it you will lose it. I was even more comfortable in the power that lived within me. Every day we are consumed with the daily tasks and responsibilities of what life must bring. The uniqueness of the pursuer is making sure that all dreams are accomplished.

Many people stop growing which causes them to stop dreaming. When I talk about dreaming this is something that can happen while sleeping and or just simply daydreaming (while awake). When you are not living, and stop expecting more you are actually choking all the life out of the dreams, you're just existing. I ask that you rebirth dreams while reading this very text. When one is able to rebirth dreams, they then become in tuned to the very thing we call living the good life. In order to awaken dreams, I had to learn that my atmosphere reflects my thoughts and transitions my dreams into purposeful and meaningful visions. And those who I allow to speak into my destiny do the same. Just think about the jobs you had and those you considered to be your mentors-are they further than where they were when you considered them to be mentors? Are the people on your job still bouncing dreams around in the breakroom? Are you able to come home for the holidays and talk about the success of a dream and the reality it has placed your lifestyle? Ask yourself, "Have I placed myself in the right atmosphere, the right people, and the right mindset to produce this dream of mine?"

Once we re-evaluate where we are and where we stand we can truly dream again.

Once we get the dreams what's next right? Well someone always told me to have a small notebook or a notepad near my bed or wherever I slept because you need to write that particular dream down. Have I kept that advice, well yes, but I haven't truly written anything down because there was one part that was missing "confidence within myself and the dream." Many times we can have a dream but never believe it can become a true lifestyle. For example, I remember having dreams of me being on stage and speaking to thousands of people, wealthy people, might I add. I didn't know where it came from, and I can't even remember what I was talking about but the audience was tuned in, and they all wanted to know more. God purposely provides vision before we can touch it. Be the producer of your own confidence, make things work and move your dreams beyond the pages of your memory. I often tell students and those whom I motivate that if you can't believe in yourself, who will? Many people will support you to accomplish your dreams but it only you who can make that dream reality. Remember, God made you, now it's your turn to make your purpose resound within the earth.

I often say a dream is one of the ways God communicates to his children. If I'm not dreaming, there is something I need to be doing to get in the right position. And if I'm dreaming crazy things- I may need to check my connections and what has controlled my mind. Again, dreaming is something you can do even when you're wide awake. It's a vision that no one can give you but the greater that's within you (your creator). Finally, I'm discovering that if I work my dream which is truly my passion, then I will constantly grow and become even better at what I do and who I am. A few months ago I was watching BET, and they were discussing the way Trey Songs got discovered. One review they captured is when Trey Songs won his first BET Music Award, and he stated: "This is what it looks like when you never give up on your dream." That particular statement woke something up in me, and now I am ready to supersede my visions and my dreams. I know now that I can do anything that I put my mind to. I didn't necessarily need that moment to wake me up, but I just needed to surround myself with motivational and life pushing moments that would put more fire under me to get the ball rolling. I can only produce my surroundings, and if I can't get out of my environment, I will work my tail off to get to the place that looks like my dreams! There has to be a certain type of PUSH that makes you live again.

Sometimes in life, we need that personal wakeup call- a moment when we are able to witness it before our own eyes. It takes a dreamer to know a dreamer, to be surrounded by visionaries and individuals who are working towards great things. If you start today, you will be closer to your ultimate dream tomorrow. Once we start doing the things we love and start seeing the growth of our passion, we will truly begin to see the seeds of supernatural wealth and before you know it you're at the place your heart desired. There has to be a shifting of the mind that will cause you to really produce in this next phase of your life. At my church, we normally do outreach on one Sunday of the month, and one homeless man said one thing that made me really think. I asked him what was the one thing he enjoyed about life, "He replied it's life, and you have to be able to adjust to what comes your way- the key is to not let life overcome you-you overcome life." Today we must overcome the very thing that test us day in and day out.

Don't confuse not dreaming as a sign from God that He has nothing to say to you. I remember my pastor Bishop Hezekiah Pressley telling me that a dry season is only to prepare you for what is coming. Even in the winter months, things have to die down so we can enjoy the flowers that grow in the spring. I have to take a moment and encourage you to stop complaining about your winter for it is only trying to prepare for your next season. Did you know that you can't take the same attitude, thoughts, and mindsets to your successful place? Better yet you can't approach a new day with an old attitude and mindset hoping to expect more opportunities, it won't work. This is why a winter season in your life is so important. What are you willing to leave, lose, and ignore to get closer to your destiny? Just the other day I was texting my mentor, Dr. Michael Magruder, he and his wife celebrated 35 years of marriage. Throughout the texted conversation he stated that 35 years of commitment takes much prayer and sacrifice. He then said he had to put his children and wife before his own needs. Sometimes in life, we have given value to the wrong things which cause us to reap unvalued worth. Success is for everyone, but everyone won't obtain the fullest potential of success because they don't want to leave anything behind. Having a mindset that is so purposed to expose your talents, strengths and weakness will challenge you and those around you to be better than you were seconds ago.

Having a mindset that will equip you for tomorrow is the most effective attitude and mindset to have. You have to set a goal to be better than you were on yesterday. Look at it like this, every day, minute and second that you're given is another opportunity that God grants you to do it right (or better) than you did before. Have you ever tried to start something and told yourself, I'll do better tomorrow? Well, can I share some news with you? Tomorrow is not promised, neither is the next second, therefore you should start today and get better at asking yourself those challenging questions.

1. Have I really used my fullest potential?

2. What does my flexibility say about my promise to reach my goals?

3. Do I have real confidence within myself?

4. Am I being REAL with myself and identifying those lazy moments?

These challenging yet purposeful questions are meant to direct you toward a better-thinking future. Again, I ask the question *"When was the last time you had a meeting with yourself, for yourself, to promote yourself?"* Today our mindset must be transformed to introduce us to the future.

What would it take for you to have the fearless attitude towards life like you had when you were a child? I often glanced at my children and how they are so fearless about making a falling down or even taking a risk at new things. As I look at them, my inner child awakens and say let's do it, let's live that fearless life. You must admit the type of faith a child has is the faith we should desire to maintain. Growing older, we allow the world to mandate how we view faith. To be honest with you having faith is a mindset. My children have faith that I will protect them, feed them, cloth them- there is not a care in the world that they have. Their mind is freed because they know that daddy is going to answer the call. That same faith is what will propel us to our destiny. Ask yourself, have I produced faith changing opportunities or have I put my trust in the worldly things?

Many business owner and celebrities have the same maker, creator, and father that we have. However, it was a mindset and or mind shifting that afforded them the opportunity to excel. If I can think it, that I shall be. More importantly, if I can speak it- the speaking shall birth the vision and effectively position me for the purpose in which I was created. Some of us are frustrated with the wrong things, we have blamed our bosses, co-workers, lack of education and student loans to the fact that we are all out of excuses. When the frustration should be pointed in our direction because we should be the owners of our success.

Life is about taking chances... If you fail the first time, take notes so you'll have a better chance to succeed the next time.

CHAPTER THREE

Identify the Why

Life is made up of crawling, falling and standing. Falling no matter what order it takes or how many times it takes for you to stand- standing should be your overall goal in life. It's not how you fall, but more importantly, it's the process in how you get back up. Today, understanding that there is a chance in which you will fall, however, don't stay down GET UP! *There is so much power in the Get Up* that will intimidate your enemies and surprise your haters. The Get Up is purposed to make you live- it is purposed to encourage you and to add value towards your goal. If you can see the fall as a prerequisite for the value in your posture, you will boost your success, and by the time you rise, again you will be seated in a purposed reality. Sometimes I think it would be cool if we could be reminded when we took our first steps, and we were trying to find our balance. It is the best way to describe us falling in the world and attempting to get back up. No one cried, or even laughed, but more emotionally, they rejoiced in our efforts to not give up. Remember that simple message today because it is your day! If you stay down, you will place limits on the power that was installed in you to stand, if you get back up you are on your way to your DREAM even better your DESTINY!

Sometimes I think about my days in school and how I dreaded a particular event and still do which is "exam day." The fact that I can't use notes or any previous exams, I can't talk to the instructor nor can I just be collaborative and work with the other classmates worries me. I studied all night and even looked at my old exams and used them as study guides. Well sometimes I would study all night long, and I would pass the test and other times I wouldn't do so well. The interesting thing is that life is set up the same exact way. Here on earth, we are given different assignments called life, dreams, goals, and purpose. With these assignments, we have been given clear instructions on how to pass the test, and we have even passed our midterm exams, but on the day of the final, the instructor (God) can't talk to you during the exam. However, you can use your notes called testimony to help you remember that since you got through that- then you can surpass your now. And normally the testimony was developed in the fall- the way you pass the test of goals, aspirations, and dreams is just to simply get back up, and when you get up it has to be with a sense of urgency. We may not have the video footage of us taking our first step but look where you are today- you're not only taking steps, but you're leaping! I just want to remind you that you can surpass your test of today.

The reason some people fall and stay down is because they have fallen on the wrong ground. You must remind yourself that you have been purposed (and chosen) to do one thing. Out of that one thing may develop a variety of gifts, talents and business opportunities but they are all under one umbrella, and that's YOU! If I am created to do a certain thing I can't devalue myself, my talents or my gifts because it appears that someone else has the same talent and or gift. There is a certain type of anointing that we all have that will draw and attract people to you. The reason we sometimes fall is because we have lost value in that purpose.

Finding the "why" in everything you do is the most effective way to discovering your purpose. Have you ever got mad about a particular thing and later on started to say to yourself- well that was connected to my why, and then question the reason you were so upset, to begin with? Everything has to be connected to your why; your friends, your job, your career, relationships, etc. If I am far removed from my why then I am far removed from my purpose which further moves me away from my destiny. Sometimes we have frustrated ourselves to the point we lose focus on the purpose and the pure "why" we even exist. You may be on a job right now or taking a class in school that is not even connected to you why – which drains the life out of you. My mom always said money does not always make you happy, so you better find something you enjoy and live rather make money and be unhappy. Let me just say this, life without purpose is the simply existing. Our goal in life should be to live life and to live it more abundantly. I want everything that is within me to have a purpose. So can I ask you a question? "Have you ever had a desire to outlive your purpose?" Outliving your purpose will cause you to be better than your why, it will cause you to live beyond the goals of today- not getting tired of trying to accomplish half of one goal but surpassing your visions, your dreams, and your aspirations. If you were to be completely honest with yourself, the reason you haven't accomplished a goal is you. It's not the money, it's not even the time. The real reason you have not met your destiny is because you are comfortable right where you are, and it will take you out of your comfort zone which you deem to be too hard for you to handle. Success is for everyone, but success isn't free- there is a price to pay, and the price is being uncomfortable.

If you know me, then one thing you will know is that I love all things purpose. I don't like sitting in meetings, and there is no purpose to it. I'm not the person that wants to meet just to meet. Even my impromptu meetings have to be about purpose or have some kind of outcome to it. Everything that you do must be connected to your purpose. I remember making several attempts at being successful- one thing I failed to realize was that it is very easy to quit, but it's a real job to go through and push yourself until you can grasp success with your own hands. We quit a lot because it's the easiest thing to do. If you really think about those successful people- they are the ones who always push every downfall, fear, and situation.

When you're able to identify your why (purpose) then you will be able to connect your right now to your future and even better your right now will introduce you to your future. During motivational presentations, I normally tell people you know when you're ready when your right now looks like your future. It doesn't mean that you have to drive the fancy cars or have the mansion but having the attitude and mindset that can handle the lifestyle you desire is all you need. It doesn't take a gifted prophet to know that I'm going somewhere because I look like where I'm going. Today shall be a day that we not only identify with our why- but that we effectively look like it. Be equipped with every fall to discover your why and have a mission to outlive your purpose so tomorrow you can be one step closer to your destiny. Take a couple of moments and write down some key things in which you know you're talented at. If you are unfamiliar with those things- I would suggest you ask someone you trust who knows you really well. Throughout the next couple of weeks create five goals for each talent and start planning strategically on how to enhance self, all while further developing the "why" in which you were created. When identifying the why it is important that you don't lose yourself in it.

Make today count for something... Stop

being lazy and stand on what your name

means.... As for me, I will be a WINNER!

CHAPTER FOUR

Train your Mind

There is so much freedom when you're able to release the thoughts, dreams, and opportunities of your mind. Everything that we dream and desire is first built in our minds. You have to tell yourself that you have the ability to FREE your mind from yourself. Take the limits off of yourself to get things done. Today I desire to free my frustrations, the thoughts of my past in doubting myself to get things completed, and the fear of the unknown. The desire to live comes with understanding that you must live beyond fear and the hurt of your past to secure freedom and a future.

Once you're able to capture the thought-provoking ideal and moment indicating that "I CAN" you are well on your way to mental freedom. This has been one of the hardest chapters to write all because I had to first free my mind from myself. Just think about it, every time you want to start a new diet, a new goal it sounds good when you first write it out- but it's the action part that makes everything so difficult to accomplish. You have to get tired of second-guessing yourself and doubting yourself over and over again to officially embark on personal and spiritual freedom. If we really knew how close we are to the breakthrough that would free our lives (financially, mentally, spiritually and personally), then we would consider taking advantage of the benefits of a freed and trained mind.

What mental distractions have caused blockage of your mind? These mental distractions are sometimes called friends, family and the most famous one is you! We have to find effective ways to free these distractions so we can be greater at what we've been called to do. The life you desire is dependent on how well you're able to free yourself from the fears of tomorrow.

The Unlocking of an Incarcerated Mind

If you were in church and I was a preacher, I would instruct you to scream "UNLOCK." But since this is only a book I guess we can settle with you just reading the word. With effective planning, you can unlock your destiny all by the building of a new mindset. The mindset is something that has the ability to capture award-winning moments. Ask yourself how have you handled what your mind has had the capacity to see? We sometimes understand that we have the power to unlock everything that we dream about which is stored in our minds, but fail to realize that *we are that power that unlocks the gift*. The training of your mind is a process and to build that process you will need to develop a strategic approach.

Have you ever thought, where would you be if you didn't allow yourself to be lazy and or backtrack? Or even consider where would you be if you freed your mind? Majority of the time our mind has been incarcerated to the dreams and aspirations of our past; the things that have held us down which won't give us access to our tomorrow. The haters, the dream destroyers are still in the back of our mind, and they have captured our tomorrow. Sometimes it's the time that has passed us by in thinking that our dream cannot be accomplished because we're too old. It's the individuals who are in your inner circle, family, and friends who doubt you of the very purpose you were created for. I have to ask the question, why are you ready to quit the very thing you're purposed to do- and even better, created for? And why is it so easy for doubt to come in-between you and destiny?

When you were created, you were equipped with purpose, innovation and the power to overcome fear. Before you were created there could have been the birthing of another human being (gift), but God chose you- therefore it should be enough to outlive your purpose. The egg in a woman is just waiting on the sperm of the man to hit so it can be produced. So many things could have happened then, however, many years later you stand as a testament that you're a survivor. We have to declare that today we are free. Jeremiah 29:11, one of my favorite scripture states "For I know the plans I have for you, plans to give you hope and a future." Within this scripture it never stated that we would know our plans- the hope is that we would have the right mindset and with the right mindset we would have faith that our desire in life is connected His plan which promotes us to have access to freedom!

Freeing our mind takes many steps and phases so we can effectively obtain all that we are purposed to have. Freeing yourself places the power back in your hands, to begin with so that we can activate the fullest potential and build up a posture that is armed to be an unmovable force. This is the day where you have to picture yourself doing better, picture yourself thinking better and see yourself living better. Recently I was at a meeting, and the presenter was trying to get faculty and staff to think about the picture that is within our heads. He instructed us to not think about the kitchen in our home- as we tried our best to take our minds off of our kitchen every time he named items that we would have in our kitchen, we pictured every item named. He later demonstrated the fact that we could affirm ourselves but people who may surround us who say negative things will block the picture of affirmation. During self-evaluation, we forget about the clear picture or even examining those objects, people and things that clutter our picture. Developing a process of a clear and clean mind takes more evaluation of self and evaluation of those who you allow to surround you.

The process of training your mind should equip you to go through your good days, and you're not so good days so you can get through everything. The main goal should be to have a DETERMINED mind. If you have ever witnessed someone who was determined to get a goal completed, someone who said they were going to and actually accomplished it. Having a mind of determination is much easier than you think- especially when you treat each new day with that new attitude and have a new approach to it. Understanding that tomorrow will be better than my today- my mind has to be unlocked and unchained by the fears of not being successful. Ask yourself this question. Where has your comfort zone done for you lately? Once we understand that moving out of our comfort zone and allowing our freedom to come within the mind is when we're able to open up and LIVE!

Majority of the times we are locked up with the keys in our hand to unlock every opportunity, every goal and every dream that is within us. It starts with the mind to start the unlocking process because if you can free your mind, you can free your purpose. Wouldn't it be easier if our purpose was on our foreheads so everyone we came in contact with could see it and grant us opportunities? Well, guess what, it does work like that. If we would allow our inner purpose to be dressed up, then our posture would showcase it.

Today could be the first day of your life if you allow "you" to work in and on your dreams. Get up and make things happen, the world is waiting for you!

CHAPTER FIVE

Keeping Your Eyes on the Prize

Never stop envisioning yourself in a better place; you deserve to live a 5-star lifestyle.

Sometimes in life, we will underestimate ourselves and our abilities to be GREAT! It is our purpose to live our life victoriously (meaning everything that I do, I will perform it on top!) Today I encourage you to be everything that you envisioned and more. I also want to encourage you to live a life that's filled with many joys, victories, and wins. When you can make your losses resemble wins in your life then you know you're on the right track. All you have to do is put a smile on your face and do one thing that places you towards your vision. You are one step away from winning in this season. Today, don't stop envisioning yourself in a better place; you are well deserving to live a 5-star lifestyle.

Keeping your eyes on the prize comes with a lot of determination and commitment to see yourself in a better place. I often think about the age I am now- I am in a better place than my parents where when they were my age. The same goes for my parents- they were and are in a better place than their parents. The world works so that our offspring can be positioned to be better than our current. If you can see the cycle, then you will notice that it is evident that tomorrow can only produce greater results than our today. There is promise in our tomorrow. Today, if we dispose of the things that attempt to block our focus, then the clear picture of grasping our tomorrow will accelerate us to our future.

Keeping your eyes on the prize gives you strength to keep going. If you can image your childhood think about the times when someone gave you a promise. I remember when my mother gave us a promise, despite how it looked the promise may have been delayed, but it was granted. Let this encourage you that sometimes the promise of a brighter future is not close to you now, you must have faith in knowing that it's in route. All you have to do is maintain a positive attitude and you shall reap the harvest of success. If you affirm yourself today that all I have been purposed to have, I shall have, you will start pushing yourself closer and closer to the prize.

The magical question, what is the prize? The prize can be many things- you actually don't have any authority in the creation of that actually "prize." Some may have to re-read this over and over again until it is revealed what that prize is. But before we were born the prize was identified- life equips you to get closer, the mindset of knowing the higher power qualifies you to obtain it. Understanding that even in the dream we are still not the person who developed that clear picture we have to keep our eye on the prize while understanding there is one who sits high and looks low who is there to help you navigate to obtain your harvest.

My first time riding an airplane I was nervous but I wanted to sit by the window. As scared as I was I still wanted to see how high we could go. I was amazed that we could see everything. I was quickly trying to gage the earth below to find things I recently visited not being able to recognize what highway was beneath me or if I could see a theme park the idea came to my head "I'm not as afraid as I thought I was". When you are on an airplane if you had to tell someone where to go and or trying to avoid accidents you could do so with ease. When you're able to have an eagle's eye view as well as having the capacity to obtain the victorious lifestyle you will be at the place you've been so desiring.

Don't allow one mistake to control your life.

Move pass the mistake and produce success!

CHAPTER SIX

Life Happens!

Get up, Get Moving and Don't Quit … This is Life!

I have a major problem when people offer you something and then leave you hanging. The approach of being stranded and having to depend on an unreliable source can leave one frustrated and giving you the desire to quit, give up and stop dreaming. There has to be an equipping of self to make sure you're prepared for the fall- we know there will be many falls in our life. My dear friend Pastor Lisa Keen once stated that there is a rock bottom on every level. With life there will be things and people that will get in the way of your success and they will come at the most opportune time. The time when you are already feeling like you're on the edge of quitting and letting go of the dream you have grasped in your hand. You have to find strategy and a network that will push you beyond your row.

Some may have thought this book would have been good just the way it is- but if we do not prepare and equip ourselves for the attack and or challenging "Life Happened" moment to occur then this book means nothing. Every chapter before now would not have any purpose unless you were fully prepared to win in every season of your life. There was a time in my life that I was very worried that I wasn't dreaming. I thought my connection emotionally, physically or personally was lost to the point that I was wondering if I would ever dream again. After consulting with my spiritual father, he reminded me of the seasons in life. There are seasons where you will have winter, spring, summer and fall.

The Strategy of Seasons

In life there will be some seasons that are only meant to purify you. It will purify you to the point where you can't hear clearly nor see the purification. But the only thing you can do is have the ability to hold on to the promise that spring time is right around the corner. The season will attempt to distract you and or get you off focus. During your winter season is set up for you to quit but to purge. Just think about what a winter season brings- Throughout the frigid weather and wind which makes people become unsociable. This causes us to isolate ourselves back in our homes under the covers until it's time to go back outside which is a dreading situation for most. If we can stay true to who we are and not lose confidence in knowing that better is coming and if we can just stand the pain of the pinching winter season then we will showcase the ability to weather the storm. Sometimes in the process of isolation we allows our thoughts to pursue our minds and lose focus in proper networking which could devalue our promise as well as default the plan in which we were working but had no idea. It amazes me how we are currently on an assignment but not able to recognize it because we can only work one piece of the puzzle. When we get to the end of the puzzle we understand that the winter seasons mattered the most.

The seasons that I'm referring to don't necessarily collide with the seasons of the year but there will be seasons when everything springs up and everything is or appears to be ok. This will be the season where it may be a lot of rain at first- every time you attempt to do things well or going in the right direction it will meet you in a raining season. The promise of your spring season is that there will be a lot of harvest if you sow seeds in the midst of the rain and in the right fertile ground. Your rainy season and timing of it only equips you to discover the beauty which is awaiting to blossom. The test and the trials of the rain is trying to see if you're really ready to handle the blooming season of your tomorrow. Psalms 30:5 says it best: "For his anger lasts only a moment, but his favor lasts a lifetime; weeping may stay for the night, but rejoicing comes in the morning". Whether you are in school or well in your career or even you're just retired make sure that you don't dwell in the situation or circumstance but have hope in that your tomorrow will be better. The uncertainty of your spring season will fully engage what is called your summer month.

The strategy of your summer season is when you're able to do the things you've desired to do. Normally if you really equipped yourself in the fall, winter and spring months then in the summer you have something to be energized about. For instance I am currently trying to start a new way of living. I go to the gym at least three times a week spending about an hour of exercising. To encourage myself my promise is that in the summer I will be more confident at the beach with my shirt off. The summer months is the time when were able to present what we've been practicing on all of the other months. We even have the ability to meet new people and add some supportive passengers to our soaring jet of success.

After having such an awesome experience with your summer season, there will be seasons when people, things, situations just fall everywhere. It appears that every direction you turn there is always something going on. Treat your fall like you just woke up in summer.

Isn't interesting that everything on earth takes advantage of the fall season except humans? The trees know when to release their leaves, the animals know when grow more fur and shed the others. I say we just follow pursuit and maybe by the next time we hit winter we will be in a more comfortable and confidently postured position where promotion becomes accustomed with who were are and wealth is our new norm. One thing that I've learned about life is that it happens, it's a revolving circle but I will not let it get the best of me. I am determined to make a difference, Today I want to encourage you to NEVER give up on life. No matter your age, current status, or position in life Get up and moving. This is only the beginning!

You can only be as successful as YOU will allow yourself to be. I'm destined to be successful in the next three months. Just watch how God does it, as a matter of fact, start counting now!

CHAPTER SEVEN

Game Time!

It's something about when the band or singer concludes the national anthem or when the referee blows the whistle, we all know that signals the game is about to begin. With life on the other hand we don't necessarily have these same signals after the doctor has spanked us and we had our first cry when we were born. Today, I want to encourage you to treat every day like it's your first. Like you were just born, meaning you have a new purpose and a new goal to reach which is for the world to know that you're alive! Especially because with every new day comes new goals, new realities and a set of new promises that can only be released if you use it properly.

Every year millions of people are excited because it gives them the opportunity to change for a new phase in their life. After a couple of weeks and for some us a couple of days, the same habits (attitudes and mindset) from the previous year meets us in the new one. The problem is that we have not placed much value on the days versus the years. In all actuality we should value the days more than the years to take full advantage of what the year has to offer. Just think a year with no days wouldn't be an actual year now would it? We have to start thinking about it being New Year's Day everyday so we are ready to stay in the game until the end. Just think about all that you could accomplish if every day that you lived you celebrated like it was New Year's Day? If you started doing your vision boards every day and reviewed the board to ensure you accomplished every goal- we could possibly see some good results.

Have you ever been a part of something and you told everyone "it's not a competition" but in the back of your head it really was? Well, I will always say "It's just a game" but my competition mode gets real. I remember purchasing a Fitbit and using it with my colleagues I couldn't get in the bed unless I accomplished my goal. My wife would come downstairs and see me walking around the basement just to meet my goal or stay in the lead. Having something that others can visible see will make you want to be better.

Staying in the game requires a lot of work and practice. If you think about a game each team is comprised with teammates who have different roles. Having a vision to win is great however having a team that will help you win would be even easier. That's why instead of having a vision board you should have a realistic *vision group* and have meetings on a regular basis to ensure that you have individuals who support you to accomplish that vision. Someone may say well my wife. husband, significant other or family is all the support I need. Well, I would have to say that sounds too much like comfort. A lot of times we feel as though someone will take our vision or dream and attempt to produce it. When a team practices everyone knows their roles and responsibilities. Take football for instance if I am quarterback I can't serve in the same capacity as the tight end or the tackle- I need others who have a different objective to do those roles. It's the same thing with your vision- have someone else who has a different way of thinking and some benefits that will help you move those boundaries and roadblocks out of your way. If I was the quarterback with the vision of a touchdown and my guard is clearing the way -I will reach my destiny faster.

To make the game impactful- look for others who are not connected to you but in key positions that can bring life to your goals. The key is building the right team that will bring long lasting results. Make up your mind that this will be a winning season for you and everything that you do will birth results and success. Understanding that life is a game and sometimes you have your championship moment and some is just the qualifying games that will push you to the next level. It makes what my dear friend Pastor Lisa Keen's statement real- every level has a rock bottom. When you start a new game the score starts at 0 and only the strongest will survive.

When you're in the game remember this is the time when you can't stop, you can't quit for this is the time when you are about to see the results of your countless practicing hours and moments. Remember people are counting on you to have an equipped posture which will change the world. Know that since you are alive today, that serves as a reminder that you still have purpose left in you to continue what you started and you're the resource someone has been searching for. Today is the day that you position yourself back in the game. You've been on the bench for a long time and today is the day where you have to pick up your goals, dreams, and plans for a better life to be the best YOU, you can be. I have dreamed too long, I have planned even longer and I am going to make today my last day to just sitting and think about my dreams but as for today, decree and declare that I am going to LIVE out my dreams! Just repeat this: *"Today, I am getting back in the game with a better mindset and more energy. My dreams are my reality, I woke up in a better day, moment, hour, and second. Today I will start discovering new paths to success that will be known to the world. I am the solution that the world is awaiting. I WILL NOT QUIT!!!!*

ABOUT THE AUTHOR

Theo Chunn lives with the passion to motivate youth and professionals to be powerful and productive citizens. It is his desire to encourage others to have a meaningful impact on how they perform academically, socially and professionally. He has been a motivational speaker since 2007. In 2009, Chunn expanded his vision by founding TCJ Motivations, Inc. Through his non-profit, he has motivated professional organizations, collegiate and high school students around the country. In 2012 He began building organizations to be premier in customer service and staff enhancement through his unique approach to developing employees and leaders. Currently, Theo is an Academic Success Counselor & Coordinator of the Freshman Male Initiative, under the division of Academic Affairs at Winston-Salem State University.

Theo is married to the beautiful Evelyn Michelle; they both have a beautiful daughter, Gracelynn Elizabeth and a handsome son Theodis "Trey" Chunn III. Chunn lives and walks by the words of Dr. Martin L. King, Jr.; "The ultimate measure of a man is not where he stands in moments of comfort and convenience, but where he stands at times of challenge and controversy."

RECOMMENDATIONS

"The roads we follow in life are filled with amazing twists and turns. Theodis Chunn has a story to tell. The roads he followed led to success and favor. He is an orator, a motivator, a family man, and a man after GOD's own heart. His path was uncertain but his future is clear. A transformative leader with a sense of purpose, his messages will inspire all and create positive change. I am proud of knowing where and how you started, but more than that, I am proud of where you are now! For you, the "Best is yet to Come."
                    -Dr. Michael Magruder

"Theo Chunn is an amazing motivational speaker. He is truly a gift of mentorship that is shown in everything he does. His book will be an uplift, guide, and will benifit anyone that is ready to make a difference."
                    - Shanta Reddick

"Theo is a proven motivational leader. He has awaken the sleeping giant within me. Everytime I encounter him I leave his presence inspired and motivated to acheive my next."
                    -Nate Atkins

"Mr. Theo Chunn is the epitome of what the world needs. He is a God fearing, intelligent, selfless black man on a mission to give back while creating more strong black men. Every person, young or old, who receives the blessing of hearing words from him is never the same after. He lights a fire of intentional encouragement and self-preservation. He takes you to the point of no return and you understand and acknowledge your calling. Mr. Chunn allows you to gratefully receive what God has favored you with. Our black men instantly stand taller, adjust their crowns and take off to do their part to save the world. Get ready...this changes everything."

                    -NaShonda Bender-Cooke, NBCT, ME

CONNECT WITH THE AUTHOR
BOOK THEO TO SPEAK!

EMAIL: THEOCHUNN@GMAIL.COM

FOLLOW THEO @TEECHUNN

(TWITTER/ INSTAGRAM)